26/9   £3.00

The Dedalus Press

The Nightingale Water

Macdara Woods

THE
NIGHTINGALE
WATER

MACDARA WOODS

The Dedalus Press
24 The Heath ~ Cypress Downs ~ Dublin 6W
Ireland

Cover Painting :
"Gulls, Sea and Sky"
by Anne Donnelly

ISBN 1 901233 64 2 (paper)
ISBN 1 901233 65 0 (bound)

Dedalus Press books are represented and distributed in the U.S.A.
and Canada by **Dufour Editions Ltd.**, P.O. Box 7, Chester
Springs, Pennsylvania 19425
in the UK by **Central Books**, 99 Wallis Road, London E9 5LN

The Dedalus Press receives financial assistance from
An Chomhairle Ealaíon, The Arts Council, Ireland.
Printed in Dublin by Colour Books Ltd

The Nightingale Water

i.m.
Seán Woods 1912 – 1980
Áine Ní Chonaill 1911 – 1999

VISITING HOURS

Sunlit ward in Pentecost
and when you wake
we'll speak

too many
heartbeats I have missed
today these weeks

and days
the sharp Epiphanies float by
too fast

to set them
down until it comes
to this — for me

a moment's pause
upon a Sunday afternoon
to watch

you sleep:
you drowse worn out
from agitation

facing off the shadows
who have
stepped across your light

Whitsuntide today
and when you wake
we'll speak

TRAVELLING

Come on now
and let's
get the little boots

the boots
are you following?

Come on Dara come on
and don't delay
if we go now we'll manage it

Can you put the sock on
the outside sock
and the boots
put the boots on the child

open the clasp
get the water out of the boots

now
do you see the leather boots
and the stuff in them

Dara that's an open-car
here with a box
that the things can be put in
and brought down

I'm here
at the receiving end
trying to poke my way around
and get little boots
and things

Have you all the little boots
now
we'll bring them across
where we might meet up
with someone else

You see what that is
now
take the child
for the last little bit now

and you see
where she is
situated
over there by the door

That's where everyone
is congregated

Come on and we'll get Frank
to put a bit of strength
on the side

Now if you could get
a little spoon
and a little nursery bowl
and feed her in the church

LATE VISITING

I am saluted by the nurse
tonight
who calls me Barret —
Barrat? Barrett? Barra?

and Billy Barrett I knew
in school —
first school I went to
Kingstown Grammar
York Road Dun Laoghaire
you the Irish teacher
I the teacher's son
on the number eight tram
but I can't ask you now
about Billy: can't ask you now
about any of it —
where we've been and where
we're headed
or what the night may hold

and terrible to note
is how with age the voice
grows querulous

and how my voice
the visitor's voice
grows querulous
from lying about life:

from refusing to admit
that never again
the mirror of ice
holding the image true
and never again to seek
release
abandon
in a catch of breath

no small death this
and no clear water in the glass

WORDS

I had a dream
last night
I dreamt I was
in Scotland
with the salmon leaping
in the water
tonight
I am strange
am I dying

and all the times
I have listened to that —
I'm done
I'm killed
I'm not a horse
If I lay down
and bled to death...

The man
in the room across
the way
with the nurse who monitors
every move
guarding
the tube in his throat
from himself
is fifty-six
the same as I am:
is alive —

and the woman
asleep
in the other bed
behind me
who breathes
on my neck in the dark
is alive —

stay with me
stay with me
don't pull away
from me
stay with me
          here
in spirit

AFTERNOON VISIT

When
Liam Creagh was dying
in the flats
his friends came in
to lure him back
with loud talk
and shouts to get up
get up
outa that
and bottles of stout:

I'm as mad
and as helpless
trying to cajole you
with words
smoked salmon
macaronics
and blackberry water —
Macdara. . .
you call
and oh. . . but
can you not

can you not
put this away

this arm
this child
all this
put them over there

and me here
my hand in yours

13

in aice leat
le mo lámh i do ghlaic

that arm
that phantom child
beyond me there
all those all that

WHEN I WAS A CHILD

When I was a child
in the children's
hospital
I saw your face
at the door
kept out
by the angry Sister
who claimed to know how a child felt
how a child's
fears could be
best allayed —
who claimed
to know better than touch
what was best
for a child
alone
in the world of the ward:

I claim
Orla claims
and what do we know —

who are we
to know how you feel
or to tell you

when or how
to wake or sleep

EVENING AFTER

Ice cold
on a summer's day
the window open
you sleep
ice-cold
at peace
        is what it
looks like
but last night's
wild party here
was disturbing and macabre:

My son Macdara
will recite a poem
My daughter Orla
will dance:

    and the sitting up
and the lying down
and the way
you can't be still —
sitting up and lying down
sitting up and lying down

15

drinking hospital beakers
of water
oxygen bubbling
in the jar on the wall
the cards
above the bed
like pictograms
in Egyptian houses of the dead:

but sedate today
i measc na sméara
with the
Kerry Spring Berries —
the Tipperary Peach
and the Purely Irish
Sparkling Spring:

Get me up
at eight
I must be up
at eight
for the party —
and the children
will be there

And it is night now —
eight in the morning
twelve hours gone

the window open
and your hands as empty
as cold as stone

ASSEMBLY DAY

The new nurse
tonight
tells me of your agitation —
I think she's not aware
that we
are nine weeks into this:

Macdara
I am feeling strange
I feel strange
tonight
stay with me here a while
Macdara

don't let me die:

I feel. . .
        uncomfortable. . .
and my chest hurts
I did it myself
and now I'm in pain

four times I did it
all afternoon
up and down
shutting the window
and on the fourth time
I did this

        all afternoon
and I have to do everything
myself —

17

you
who can't leave the bed

The nurse
asks you how you are —
I'm well and you?
      Well thank you
and. . . *I*
should have said
thank you
too
. . . *my manners*. . .

She's a pet
says the nurse

a pure pet only

TIME OUT

Today in Ranelagh I see
the stooped librarian
who juggled the books of youth
for me
      and across the street
to the manner born
the ghost of Justin O Mahony
dark and bearded and young

Four in the afternoon
and the headaches start
again

I see
the great ones gather
just outside my vision
novelists teachers painters
singers
young Guards in acid-yellow
jackets — joggers bursting
out of Art Show shirts

and my red-haired woman
from the fish-shop
ten years older
picks up letters from the Post

AND TONIGHT

Tonight
I find you asleep
again
head placed mighty
on the pillow
lips set firm
in hard command —
and on the ledge
above the bed
a note in Gaelic taught by you
to the woman
who writes it now:

this afternoon
you called for help
from anyone who
came to mind:

It is not fair
to let me die like this
you said to Orla
send me someone sensible
someone good
someone
who cares
and who can do something:

She tells me too
the news is
that you walked today
with help
but walked
and that you need your shoes:

runners will do
they say
with no irony

runners
that hurt your feet before —

in South America
and Galway
in Egypt and Australia

that arrogant —
my feet are perfect

you should have
the handmade boots
from Naas

Mrs Pike

Mrs Pike
the woman breathing
in the next bed
died today
at seven in the morning —
on her 90th birthday
plus a day
God rest her

there are too many
poems
in this twilight place —

The woman
in that bed tonight
whose name
I shall learn
asked me after she
dropped her glass —
who owns
that big dog?

Robert

Don't bully me
Hedli
I'll not be bullied
said Robert MacBryde
as we lay
in a summer field
at Timoleague

in the 'sixties
watching
tiny tractors climb
up and down the hill
across the valley

Don't bully me Hedli
I'll not be bullied —
that and:
observation is my business

Death beat him
down
in Leeson Street
a few years after
bullied him into the ground
with all his
changeling gifts:

And there's no way
round it
no going back
no way there
sweet man or not —

just to jump and catch
to catch and hold
the image
for a moment
high above the street —

And see just now where
a hearse goes by
        a hearse with coffin
and no cortege

STRUCK

Niall was right
when he said
you had fallen from the horse
like Oisín —
touched
the mortal earth:

don't tell me
any more
new information

all I can do
is make little remarks

about you and me
and
a few others

not that I'm
not interested. . .

it's just
    my head. . .
and my mouth is parched:

    come in
closer now
and talk the way we talk:

Does Niall
ever ask for me?

and there's no way to tell you
it was Niall who said

that you fell
from the horse —

struck-down in early morning
April

like Saul
lay blinded in the road

XIV

Do you know who
I called out for

    in the night

My mother

Margaret Teeling
      McConnell

and I was thinking
of my home

I didn't know
how much I liked
my home

there was always heat
and the open fire:

and
Máire Mhac an tSaoí
is a good poet also

a very fine poet
    after all:

Strapaire fionn
        sé troithe ar airde
Mac feirmeóra
        ó iarthar tíre,
Ná cuimhneoidh feasta
        go rabhas-sa oíche
Ar urlár soimint
        aige ag rinnce

that's what we were
        country people

But
don't tell me things
that have me thinking

I'm
down down down
am I dying:

I kept thinking that
all day
and I'm quite content
because
I feel so sick:,

Do you see this room

this was my old
sitting-room

I never thought

       to   have
such unhappy
   days there

Lord look
     mind me now
I need minding
this evening

XV

I haven't got anything
           no
all this
        put this
put them

and cover them up

here   take this

here take this
       take this
       the child

take this
   this arm
put it over there

the child
and cover it up

PAUSE

There was time still
for looking
in the
full-length mirror
in the rehabilitation room

for reaching
for the coloured therapy rings

for waving
at the glass
to a stranger from
the past

still time for heartbreak

as hearts are broken:

you called me baby doll
a year ago

I never understood
when I heard
you sing that. . .

once only
half a hundred years ago

a cablegram from another world:
and
the nightingale singing

in Berkeley Square

PATIENCE

Orla tells me
how the nurses said last week
you drive them mad
but they like you

This afternoon
you drove me mad —
and when I believed I didn't
was time to leave

XVIII

If I had someone
                        to
take me and walk me
I could get up

or I'll have to
        get out in the road

to get someone to help me

to move

to get down
and put on my shoes:

EVENING LIGHT

In silhouette
against
the evening light
a figure locked
in a private myth

sitting up
in bed
pushing the rocks
of time
from your knees

a warm south
wind
blows in today
from the sea
and oh just once

to see you lying
back or
lying down to sleep
just that —
to be done

with the task
of giving up —
I'd wish you absent
to be gone
from this

to be taking your ease
ag ligint do scíth
in feathers
of ducks
like Eibhlín Dubh

not tantalised
at the end so
pushing shards
of hope and faith
around a bed

XX

I am very sick
Am I going to die?
I'm finished here
I hate this place
I cannot bear it
I can do nothing
I cannot bear it
I can't go on

Am I going to die?
I am dead
I can't do anything
I can do nothing

Better to die
And have done with it

SECOND NIGHT-STROKE

The force of
gravity
that struck again
on wings
of blood
swooped upward
to the brain

hit random
home
and terrible
again:
turned round and round
and struck
again:

the purposeful
assassin
locked into
the genes
to flesh the circle out:

hits home
in the extended
time
of night

stretched thin
to find us

trusting
open
naked or asleep

JULY TWELFTH

I woke this
morning
after three hours sleep
to hear the news
and felt the breath
of evil
in my house

In
Ballymoney
in the night
three children
firebombed
burnt to death:

the Devil walked
abroad
among the drums
and preachers'
talk

incited madmen
in the blood

and dark
this hateful week
of rhetoric
to leave
a dirty smoke-stained wall
his monument:
three children
inside
burnt to death

and what can I do
but name them
say
their names again
for meaning:

Richard
Mark and
Jason Quinn

that they were here
as we
identical
and various

may
this preserve us
at the end

          this day
and all our days

from giving up on hope
from giving in

to weariness
despair and weariness

from failing life
through weariness

XXIII

I thought of Jack
            again
      that poem

Urlár soimint
      aige ag rinnce

      the cement floor
            and you wouldn't
have a stitch
of a shoe on you after:

and show me that...
            pullover
      I used to put buttons
            like that
      and the lace
on Siabhra's socks:

            and that's the shawl
            that Redwan's mother sent
            from Libya

it was good
of her:

last thing
tonight before we leave

we ask the nurses
for a note

to take us quickly through
tomorrow's cordon

around the cyclists
of the Tour de France

Is táim le seal na diaidh
O chaill me mo chiall le nuachar

SMALL HOURS

Things we forget
    to record
lost like
    all the songs
    and poems
in one head

things reminding us
of themselves

    record me
    record me
write me down

    the horse I hear
    each night
I lie awake

    lonely
    hoof-beats
    in the Ranelagh Road

RIDDLE

Today
on
St Mac Dara's Day
a changed
dimension

there is
an absence

some other
doorway opening

a road
I do not know

. . .as I came over
a windy gap
I met my Uncle Davy

The place
we occupy —
in you
I recognize the tilt
and setting
of the shoulders:
the family

not one of them
could die in peace

. . .I laid him down
and sucked his blood
and left his body aisy

walking the land
a preparation

in the stance
and in the head

in sleep
a hand upon the bed-rail

gone
the road that leads us

out of town

XXVI

you know
           where
      you are. . .

Who's going to come with me?

      put me to sleep

If I could get to
sleep

      put me to sleep
tell her
she's minding me
      put me to sleep

SUNDAY AFTERNOON

Suddenly terribly
shockingly awake
at 3.30
and yawning
eyes wide open
staring at me

wasn't I mad to sleep
what should I do now

    I thought I'd be up
long ago

What time is it?
              Half- past three
Eight o'clock?
              Half-past three
Half-past eight
    well I'm just going to lie
here for a bit

then I'll get up

and then you can lie here

Dara
    I can't get up
What'll I do?

Can't you just go down
    and get yourself together

Listen
 do you know what
let's just stay on in bed
and we won't get up at all

What time is it . . .eight o'clock?

I'm just going to lie here
and not bother

and we won't get up at all
could we do that?

Oh Dara
I'm not able to get up
what'll we do?

Let's not bother to get up

just lie here
 till morning

Oh Dara
I've a dreadful pain in my arm

 I can't get up
 do you know what...
since I got that stroke
 I'm not able to get up

you'll have to get me up

You know
 you don't stir either –
just stay in the bed

42

and the man
in the room
across the ward
who spent
so long so far away
lying there
for weeks
with a pipe in his throat
is awake now too:

awake and clear
and that's the difference
and looking over
his nurse's
          shoulder
is reading
her shiny magazine

Dara
        I'm not able
                to get up
oh come on
I'm not able to get up

just stay in bed
        for the whole day

MONDAY

Where have the songs
gone?

the gift of tongues

to be broken like this
occurs once only

she's delighted to see you
says the student nurse

but I see the agitation beast
come back

that frightful stranger
taking over

and we are
       broken
       eaten up
       devoured
by agitation

can you help me
can you help me
to get a book
to get a book
and I'm not able

we have rehearsed the parts
and our identities
anxieties
are interchangeable

Dara
> *have you a book*
> *I could give to someone*

> *I can't make a book*
> *because everyone expects me*

> *you have one done*

I'll give you that

> *Could you do that*
> *that's what we'll do*

Someone
> *is making me do things*
> *and I'm not able*

> *and they say yes you can*
> *and I'm only pretending*

I'm not able
> *to do anything*

> *will you tell somebody*
> *and tell them not to be at me*

HIATUS

In this pre-thunder
yellow light

before the summer storm
I see my mother

now in effigy asleep
at last

imperious
head thrown back

a Pharaoh
in a poem of mine

from twenty years
and more ago:

strange how things
come home

come back come round
again —

those Egyptians in the
X-ray pictures

yellow hair
combed back from brow

the sea-girl
out of Keegan's fish shop

saved once again by
Ruggiero

or the Norman knight
on catafalque

I saw
that day in Vezelay

these skip
the circuits of the brain

redraw
the rules of memory:

And someone else
will come in time

to scan
these dreadful months

our crooked span of pain
and doubt

reliving
how they fell in love got drunk

or made love on a summer
night

saw the past come round
again

or saw their
children's children born

SEDATION

Dara
> *do you know what*

> *there's a big egg*
here in the bed
> *with me*

> *and it's too big*

Dara
I don't know what I'm saying

will you
> *stay with me*
will you
> *let me alone*
don't leave me

I want to go asleep
> *how should I do that*
my foot is cold
> *how should I avoid that*

will I go asleep
> *will I*
> *or should I keep awake*

Oh Dara
> *hold onto my hand*

and give me
> *my hand*

I have these strange things
              on me
hello
hello
should I
         show myself a bit

and don't go asleep now
                   pet

take away that thing
that. . .
         look
and don't let it use

            watch out
            the nettles

            I'm tempt

now don't. . .I

oh. . . I was
where

ROLES

We have all
become

like children
in the park

when I was
young

who played
a game

of then you
must

and then
I must

and then you
must

and now
the nurses say

they read
my Whitsun

poem to you
at night

to ease
the agitation

sometimes
in the

small hours
two a.m.

MINDSCAPES

You dreamt
you were left in a field
all night
in a shed in a field
a bothán
on the Old McConnells'
land:
the ones who hid
the half-moon parings
of their nails
and their folded locks
of hair
in hollow places
in the walls:
but which of us
wouldn't
prefer to lie out
in a field at night
to be gone from here
and wake with leaves
about the bed
recalling mysteries
the old road
underneath a ditch
the line
between the farms
a rough-flagged path
where mushrooms grew
from stones: as I
remember it
you warn me now
of nettles
stinging plants

and the cure
grows near the cause —

I think of this
and walk
into the sea today
along an
eighteenth century road —
the lines
beneath the earth

the rowan tree
the human heart

the cure
beside the cause

XXXIII

Dara
        son
will you give me a hand

            I don't
            know what to do
                    love

will we ever get it right

Dara
        oh Dara
what will I do

it's not right

Dara
    I didn't get it done
    will you
            tidy up the place

Come on and get
            up
    oh pet it's stuck

I've got to
    get up now
    and get things ready

I can't get up
    I can't do anything

    will I stay in bed

APPEARANCES

Asleep you all look
almost undamaged

no trace of terror

your companion
suffering. . .
fluid of the lung
and
a touch of Alzheimer's. . .

yawns
and shows
a perfect set of teeth
before closing her mouth
into a smile once more

asleep
she looks in charge
not
the poor creature
crying out

sussuration
of voices
from the nurses' station

and such a
normal sound
the clearing of the throat —
sound of someone
in control

And how safe sleep looks —
acceptable face
of death it's not

XXXV

Orla
put me to sleep

Come on

Eiléan
    and put me to sleep

Orla
    Eiléan —

Dara, Siabhra
    put me to sleep
    I'm all sore

    put me into
    a nice sleep

Come on
    the rest of my sleep now

    put me to sleep
    and put me
    to sleep

    just put me to sleep
    and let me sleep

    and then

    and put me to sleep

PIETA

preserve us now
from merely
going through the motions

and let us know
that we are real

we must all be
named
there must be a record
that we've been here
that we were

and occupied a space
that we
inhabited the years
we spent here

that the space we occupied
remains
essentially our own

that two bodies
cannot
occupy the same space
at the same time
their tragedy

we were
we are
the hollow figures
that remain
inside the lava
the spaces
in the pumice stone

are what
we leave behind

the Pompeian shapes
we occupied

imprint imprint
smudged
      line
or not
record me

XXXVII

All of that
      is lost to me now

      is a light slip
          of a dress
      not for anything

      but hot
         hot
      white hot

So stay with me pet

      I want to just
      have my mouth open

        let me out now pet
mind me
      love

mind me

mind me while I'm here
in the bed

FEARS

I was frightened
to see you frightened
that last time
in Italy

when your skin dried
and cracked
in the dust and heat

I noted it a premonition

and this is worse
this cracking and giving

in
the plank of reason
yes

and it frightens me to
see you frightened

nó Gallilee
          go Gaillimh

agus
ná bíodh faitíos ort
go bhfeicfidh tú

faitíos orainne
as the men in the turf-boat
said

to calm you
seventy years ago

on the rough seas to Aran

XXXIX

Dara
        will we have
        four roses
        or five

Where is Orla..
                is the
        whole of her there

        Tell me
        Dara
        has Orla money

        for the roses

        how many roses
        have we

        can you
                get
        the two of me
                together

Don't

    say you can

    if you can't

FRIDAY

I looked forward
today
to bringing you
news of my travels

Séard dúirt sí Raifterí
tá m'intinn sásta
Ach gluais an lá liom
go Baile Ui Laí

to tell you about
my trip to Achill
how the journey
we made
through the night together
is famous

An cuimhin leat an oíche
at two in the morning
from Mayo to Dublin

only a few short years ago

    I'm tired
    I'm tired

I'm too tired now
        shut it

        shut it

        shut the shoe

SATURDAY

Come on
          Come on

 Come on
          how long
          till morning

an hour
          an hour more

          an hour
 is it —

          is it time

          could you tell me

          when it's time

Dara
          will you
          tell me the time

61

I don't know
anything

And I look out
through the window
at
the evening sun
reflected

and
the free-moving
far away
marvellous lights
of ships
passing Howth

DISCOURSE

hold my hand
        for a minute

                Come on
                till I tell you

                we want to be careful

and have
        the knee-shirt

hang it
        in front of the fire

Did you
        put the cakes on
did you

Take that thing
                of mine
        that's on the knife

        I'll put it on
        when yours is off

We need the
        basin again

the basin
        of water
        that's outside
                again
        and the white cloth
        for the tea-pot

Dara
        I want you to
                put down
                your spoon
in the tea-pot

        won't you
                won't you
and then. . .

and then
                put
                the sugar bowl
in the tea-pot then

63

and I'll put my feet
in it
and keep it closed
and nice

then do that
put the
do

put the
cloth on each
you
oh please
do that for me now

don't kill me

Will you
put them
in the boots first

your boots
and then put
the socks

the more
socks boots

and you
can do
the buttercup

will you like that

Put me
    one foot
    on the boot
    for a while
and then it will hold it

        afterwards
        will you
        get the feet
            off the boots

        and have them baked

        will you

        I mean
            the feet
        in the other boots

        you know

You take the stuff
            off
        my tea-pot now
        with
        the stuff

Dara
        Come on

        Come on here
                    now

        and cut off my hair

come on now
        and do it

stop
        eating. . .

and put my
                knives and forks
        up
                to my mouth

won't you do that

        good boy
        do that now

and I might go to sleep

US THEN

These were not
the sounds of my childhood
of the ornamental singing
this is not how you were

Speaking in tongues
with Madame Maud Gonne
in the Roebuck Palace
of the Quicken Trees

Now they say you ramble
when you name the names –
for the people you call on
are dead and gone

Agus cabhair ni ghairfead féin
something else I've learned –
Dar an leabhar dá ngairinn
níor ghaire-de an ti dhomhsa

But you and I forever
in the snows of forty-seven
making our way
to the number Eight tram

And didn't we take pride
in the Old Road to Tara
that crossed our parcel
of no-man's-land

THURSDAY

>   *All the places*
> *I go*
> >   *that's why*
> >   *I'm tired*

> *Can I go now*
> >   *Can I*
> >   *Can I*

> *and put on my shoes*

can I
can I

and then slow
blind questing creatures

fronds
hands

pick up my spectacle-case

pick hopelessly
at the bedclothes

women on hillsides
and slag-heaps:

picking coal
at the shore

picking sea-coal

gleaning and garnering:
raking clinkers

women
picking through the dead lands

BLIGHT

Asleep
in
the fever of a week
of funerals
carnage from the Omagh bombing
this
has been a dreadful time

revulsion:
there has been
a blight
upon the land
all summer

but it isn't enough
now
to say that —

revulsion
itself
is no plan for living

Increase Of
Racist Attacks
In Dublin
          where
is it from —

I have no words

blood and water
light and air

escape to the hillside

a few
my sister among them

go back to the sea

Beadsa im shí gaoithe
romhat shíos ar na bánta

SEEING

Signs that come
on the wind

burrs
and twigs and leaves

the signs your mother
would read
in a dog's coat

there is no cure
for any of this

DISTANCE

from close-up
in the room with you
to now
beyond the corridors
and paths:

In Italy
tonight I'm looking backward
from a distance:

away from you
for a week
I hear
I see
a woman
shouting in a room

Come and help
help me
oh
hello hello

come and help me
hello hello

to everyone
and none

and no one stops

come on
come on and help

and no one stops

come on

DISCOVERIES

Indifference
not hate
is the opposite of love

a phrase
in after-dinner talk
in La Goga

The eye has its rights
said Paul next
day over lunch:

and maybe so –
But what of
the fierce corollaries?

Again I'm walking
down
the corridor of dread

today and thinking
of shouts
in the graveyard

the digger of graves
in Meath
who'd shout to raise the dead

. . . glory be to the
and may perpetual now
and forever

expectations
of golden whiskey

light
shine in showers
upon them. . .

I don't
feel indifference

some kind of
freedom maybe

now I've learned

dread settles
in the stomach

while fear
fills up the throat

RETURN

The old
bifocal look

meant
to make me feel guilt
but I don't

afternoon siesta
Dublin. . .

5.40

all parties
sleeping
except for us

So quiet
today. . .

And who
are those two women
above the bed

in a fairytale
wood
in fairytale clothes

lace-up shoes
and pinned-up skirts

picking roses
for a wicker basket

What was it
      you said last month. . .

        has Orla
            money
        for the roses

        and how many

        how many
            roses

        have we

YOUR MOTHER

The last time your mother
my grandmother
walked into Athboy
a man working in the plantings
cut her a stick
a cane for her journey
her last:

all her life she had prayed
for three days
warning of death:

a vessel burst in her brain
as she walked
past the wall
of the undertaker's yard:

she died
in a friend's house
36 hours later

in her pocket
two letters

in her glasses-case
money

for Masses: for
the Repose of her Soul

and peace among
her quarreling children

LATE VISIT

come here to me
and comfort me

I'm strange
for weeks

I have been rambling

and blathering
always blathering

but now I'm right

is this the madness
breaking out

the madness
and my head
my head is going to burst

tell the people
in the house
to come on up

and comfort me
I need to be
comforted
about the face

LII

I have had
terrible dreams

and experiences
all these weeks

and you. . .
I dreamt last night

that you
          were dead
that I was old
and strange
and going to die

that you were dead
          and I
was going to have a baby

          wasn't that
a terrible dream to have?

BREAK

Yesterday
was a balmy day
sunlight too
and we talked
of this strange abundance of houses
your house
and my house
the house in the hospital
the bothán
in the field
the house that is the hospital
and a room
a woman locked you into
once
in Meath

the unrealities
we make —
to live with
our worries and our urgencies

It wasn't right
you said
for my uncle
(your brother
who is long since dead)
to be sleeping
with young women

and you see them
over there
leaving his bed

young women
besides
who are beautiful
and young
so young and beautiful
and
much too good
for the likes of him

LIV

There's a whole
  lot of stuff
  gone away . . .

I'm going
   to go away

if you don't go away

   I'm very peculiar

   You're going away from me
                              pet
   oh yes you are

   don't do that to me

Dara
   Dara

   don't leave me now

WEDNESDAY

Mouth pursed:
you sleep
a frowning sleep

the new woman
in the next bed
asks me my name

Your mother
needed you
she tells me –

She called for you
all night

INSIGHTS

like a lizard
I need sunlight
in the morning
to
warm my blood

I begin
to
hate to hear
my name called out

begin to hate
the sound
of my own name

MONDAY

My face and all
is as sore as a boil

bed manual:

to raise
to lower
to arrest descent

taboos:

scavengers
hyenas
bone carriers

young men
with butchers' knives:

what
is the common human
factor

but
green stalks:

green
garbage-stalks

the column of
the spine

a stalk
into the brain. . .

the
broken stem
le roseau

reed

qui pense

II

NOVEMBER

November
and the tail-end of a hurricane
it seems strange

at the end of it all

at the last home
I wait here to welcome you

grey day
at the unexplored end
of Ranelagh –

down by the brimming river
I heard. . .
there is a tree
that grows aslant a brook

where murderers
lure children
disused railway tracks
back lanes
and river paths

we drown
and all our stories
wash
down-river to the sea

I must
take up the story once again

In nineteen forty-six
or seven
in Pembroke Street
you said
you would humiliate me
for taking
a couple of walnuts
from a shop display

and many a time you did

one way and another
of all mothers
one's own is the maddest

Will you
embarrass me today –

what can I say
for you
long since
gone into
a country of the mind
where I can't speak
protect you
or protect myself

HERE

In the last place

sounds of the night

voices raised
protestation
mutter
as of Rosaries

scuff of my feet
in the corridor

patterns of sound

coughs
clearing of phlegm
sighs
and protest

sleeping sounds

and the
oxygen hiss – so gentle
numinous

as candle-light

THERE

From next door
raised
a querulous angry
old woman's voice

". . . Cow Cow
What are you saying
cow for?

There's no cows here
unless you're the cow

And I know what kind
of cow you are. . ."

THIS

This is what people do
cry out
go on journeys in the night

Let me go now
and it'll be
my last caprice

and do you know
what I would love

is water from the well

what I would love
to have
is some of that
nice
nightingale water

I write it down

as writers do

do texts destroy each other
and themselves?

LXII

I'll never forgive you
Dara
for letting me die like this:

but
I don't need forgiveness
nor do you

you poor old broken creature in the end

we have come through
pity and terror and fear

it's done

the walls are down
on whatever it is

and when you go it is gone

WE

We are the whisperers in
the shadows
we talk of times-past signposts
the Granard Bus
Joe Duffy radio programmes
the present scandals
brown paper bags and envelopes
stuffed with cash –
fifty grand the going rate
for an item of chicanery
a hundred and eighty thousand
to keep the Celtic Helicopter
flying. . .

This is the kind of stuff
we mention
rehearse in whispers
while we wait
keep vigil and wait
for a change in the breathing
and that's the kind of affair
it is in the end
after all the shouting and roaring
the bravado and the baroque
to be getting ready
like swallows on the
telegraph wires in Autumn

Frowning a little
before the plunge

to open the wings and off